This book is intended to offer advice. It does not guarantee that if the advice is followed, the reader will have success in securing any job that has been applied for. Neither the author nor publisher can be held responsible should the advice in this book be followed and no position is forthcoming. Note that all names and CV examples given are fictitious. Any resemblance to any real person is purely coincidental.

The essential guide
for today's jobseekers

HOW TO GET THAT JOB!

Lorraine Mills

Matador
9 Priory Business Park,
Wistow Road, Kibworth Beauchamp,
Leicestershire. LE8 0RX
Tel: 0116 279 2299
Email: books@troubador.co.uk
Web: www.troubador.co.uk/matador
Twitter: @matadorbooks

ISBN 978 1800462 137

British Library Cataloguing in Publication Data.
A catalogue record for this book is available from the British Library.

Printed and bound in Great Britain by 4edge Limited
Typeset in 11pt Ten Oldstyle by Troubador Publishing Ltd, Leicester, UK

Matador is an imprint of Troubador Publishing Ltd

Contents

Introduction

The aim of this guide is to give support to anyone looking for a job, regardless of qualifications, position, experience, or job sector.

If you are unprepared, your interview will end up being stressful for you. So, what is the point of putting yourself into a stressful situation repeatedly because you choose not to improve your presentation and interview techniques?

Certain hirers may decide to conduct all stages of the interview process via video interviews. Other hirers could offer a first stage video interview, and if you are successful, a series of face-to-face interviews may follow. Some hirers may even resort to only offering face-to-face interviews. Two or three rounds of interviews to just one company may be needed, and if you are unsuccessful, you will have to make fresh job applications elsewhere and repeat the whole interview process again before a position is eventually secured.

Interviews can be expensive for the interviewee. There is the cost of purchasing and maintaining a suitable outfit, which nowadays you are less likely to wear to work on a regular basis because most people in the workplace 'dress down'. And then there is the expense of travelling to and from any face-to-face interviews you may have.

So, why not get your interview technique right first time by following the useful tips mentioned in this guide? Hopefully, you will then stand a much better chance of securing one of the positions you are applying for sooner rather than later!

How To Get
That Job!

You know you can get and do the job. You want the job, so why give the opportunity of getting the job you want to another candidate? Whether you are at junior level, senior management level, a graduate or school leaver, everyone has plenty to offer in the workplace. In this competitive job market, it is important that you project your personality, so you stand a good chance of getting offered a job.

Make sure you go to your interview with PURPOSE and be:

- **P**unctual
- **U**p to date
- **R**eassured
- **P**repared
- **O**rganised
- **S**mart
- **E**nthusiastic

And – GET THAT JOB!

This book is only a guideline to job hunting. It is down to personal choice as to how you decide to present yourself and your CV when it comes to looking for and securing a new position.

1   Your curriculum vitae is your ticket to an interview

The content and presentation of your curriculum vitae (CV) needs to be of a high standard. Thanks to the power of technology, everything about your CV must be right first time before it is sent to prospective employers. If a CV of poor quality goes out to a company via an online application, it may not be possible to recall your CV. It will have been received by the hirer and this could make it difficult to reapply using a better, more informative CV.

So, try and get your CV right first time.

It is an obvious thing to mention but spelling mistakes in a CV are a disaster. If you have any number of spelling mistakes in your CV, the chances of being invited for an interview may be greatly reduced.

Job seekers often misspell words in their CV. Please see the correct spellings for some of those words below:

- Stationery
- Driving Licence
- Business
- Environment
- Mathematics
- Curriculum
- Grammar
- Cello
- Ensuring
- Successful
- Liaise
- Colleague
- Definitely

Just to be on the safe side, it might be an idea to ask someone you know to go through your CV with you before it is sent out.

A two-page CV for an *experienced applicant* is more likely to hold the interest of the person who is hiring. A three-page CV might just be too long.

A one-page CV for a very *junior-level applicant* may be enough. If you have been to university, it could be an idea to mention the modules studied if they link in with the role for which you are applying. Also, any weekend work, holiday jobs or work around your studies are always worth a mention. It will not matter if that work ranges from retail/hospitality to an office role; at least you will get a chance to detail your skills and responsibilities.

For example, if you studied finance but some of your modules covered marketing, this would be good to mention if you are applying for a marketing role. In other words, focus your CV so it is either relevant to the position you are applying for, or, if you are applying 'cold', for the next role you want to do.

Detail the duties you performed in your role. Bullet points are good to use, but there can sometimes be a danger that, while the point is being put across, a shortcut version of duties can indicate limited experience. So, use bullet points carefully.

When it comes to outlining work experience in your CV, target the areas that you know will get your CV noticed.

You may wish to create a Video CV to accompany your application, but it should not replace a traditional CV. There is no guarantee that a hirer will decide to view a Video CV.

Remember to update your LinkedIn profile.

2   School leavers, college leavers and recent graduates

Whether you have just left school, college or are a new graduate, if you lack work experience and you are presented with some work, ideally paid, then seize the opportunity, even if it isn't in your chosen field. It is important to gain work experience so you can develop a more detailed CV; this will help you get the result you want when it comes to any future job applications.

If you are looking for your first permanent role, make sure you familiarise yourself with your chosen area of work and that you are well prepared for your interviews.

- Try not to feel daunted by the interview process.
- Treat each interview opportunity seriously.
- Try not to let any negative talk among friends about how difficult the job market is, make you feel like giving up your job search.
- Believe in yourself and you will eventually get a job.

If you follow the personal presentation and appropriate CV guidelines in this book, as well as many of the other tips that are mentioned, you will hopefully gain job success.

3 CV profile

A profile in your CV can be a really good way to immediately introduce your skills, experience and personality to the person hiring. Or it can be a way to give focus to other positive areas about you if your work experience is not of relevance to the job that you are applying for, or if your general experience is limited and a bit 'all over the place':

- Include a profile at the top of the first page.
- Ideally the profile should be no more than five lines long. However, a shorter profile can sometimes be just as effective.
- A profile needs to emphasise any relevant skills you may have for the vacancy for which you are applying.
- If you are applying 'cold', then your profile should indicate your passion for the type of role you desire.

There can often be a crossover when it comes to certain industries, so your profile will need to be relatively precise. For example, if you are applying for a job in technology and you have a background in property, make sure you emphasise the sort of exposure you have had to technology.

Similarly, if you are applying for a marketing position, then specify your interest in marketing in your profile. The same will apply if you are putting your CV forward for a role in public relations.

As this will be the case with any sector you are going for, it may be worth having several versions of virtually the same CV, with an appropriate profile emphasising your specific skills, so that you can target the relevant role you are applying for effectively. This will enhance your chances of at least getting offered an interview. There is no point sending a CV for a marketing position that has a profile header indicating your passion to get into public relations:

- Your profile should indicate your dedication to your chosen subject, and why you feel you would be a good employee for the position applied for.

- The profile should reflect the type of role you are seeking and that should fall in line with the role applied for.
- Certain words and phrases, if appropriate, are a plus to mention, for example: hard-working, focused, dedicated, committed, team player with the ability to also work unsupervised, quick learner, professional, multi-tasker, experienced, motivated, bright. If you mention such words in your profile, make sure you follow up by giving solid examples in the main body of your CV to justify why you describe yourself in such a way.

If you studied Geography at university, or you left school or college with other types of qualifications, and you are applying for a junior position in a sector that is of particular interest to you, a profile at the top of your CV will be helpful, because it will engage the interest of the person who is hiring.

Ideally, your profile should match the job you are applying for. It might be good to briefly mention the sort of personality you have as well.

- For example, if you have limited work experience, your profile could read:

  Bright, ambitious individual with a keen interest in marketing determined to secure an account executive position within a progressive marketing agency. Enthusiastic fast learner with excellent people skills and the ability to work individually or as part of a team.

- The profile doesn't necessarily have to be about what you have done in previous employment, because what you have done or are currently doing in a job may not be what you want to carry on doing.
- Create a profile with convincing words if you lack experience in the area you are approaching.
- Even though you may have had years of experience, a sharp profile emphasising your title and indicating where your current strengths lie, could help make your job application more successful. For example:

  Sales Manager with excellent skills in...

Or:

  Finance Director with strong exposure to...

4 CV content

If you have been out of college or university for, say, a year, then after working in several temporary roles you decide on your chosen career, how on earth do you persuade a company to give you a chance and employ you?

Well, the first opportunity you may have of persuading a company to invite you for an interview will be with a CV that gets the point across, projects who you are, what you have to offer and the sort of role you are seeking. You may also have to supply a supporting cover letter with additional information outlining why you would be suitable for the role:

- Your education/qualifications are probably going to be on the first page of your CV if you are at junior level and fresh out of school, college, or university.
- If you are a more experienced candidate your education/qualifications should go on the second page.
- A strong profile will be of great importance, because it will support your experience, or if you lack experience, the profile should outline your personal strengths.
- It is your choice if you decide to include your home address and/or date of birth in your CV, but for reasons such as location and security, it might be better to leave them off.

Do not give misleading information in your CV about your qualifications, or where you studied. For example:

- If you are currently studying for a degree, or left without completing the course, do not put down that you have a degree in the qualifications section of your CV. Similarly, if you studied at Oxford Brookes University, do not put in your CV that you studied at Oxford, unless you really did study at Oxford University!

It is always a good idea to look into doing an evening or distance learning course that may be relevant to your chosen area of work, as this could add weight to your application:

- The main body of your CV should contain your work experience. This will apply whether you have GCSEs or a degree, or are a shop assistant, a secretary, a bookkeeper, or an accountant.
- It is a good idea to mention achievements and to follow up with relevant examples of how you made a difference in your current role and how those achievements could be of benefit in your next role.
- If you studied business at university and you are applying for a marketing post, then put down the modules you studied if they include marketing.
- Also, the work experience gained during an industrial work placement is vital, so mention as much as you can, because this will boost your CV content. That will be most important, especially if you have recently graduated.
- If you left school with GCSEs or A levels and drifted in and out of different jobs, you will have to detail all the work experience you gained, however varied.

You may find that, after a few years of being in the workplace, your CV is going off on a tangent, so it would be good to sort your career focus via your CV:

- IT skills should be mentioned under a separate heading.
- Hobbies and interests outside the workplace are always vital to include in a CV as they can create more of a conversation between the interviewer and interviewee. Talking about them can break down any barriers and help overcome nerves. They can also create synergy between you and the interviewer.
- It is a good idea to put your name, and possibly your email address in a footer at the bottom of the second and, if applicable, third page of your CV, then the hirer will not get it confused with a CV belonging to someone else.
- Dangerous sports are not good to mention. Such activities may compromise insurance cover that could be part of the benefits offered by the company hiring. You could come across as being a liability.
- For obvious reasons, it might be better to avoid mentioning any political preferences you may have, or activist groups you may belong to.

- The football club you support may be best left off too. If the hirer is a Chelsea supporter, an Arsenal-supporting candidate may stand less of a chance of being hired!
- Unless your aim is to work for a travel company, avoid talking about travel and being 'passionate' about travel. This may indicate that you are a bit of a 'fly-by-night' and that after six months you will be off trekking the Himalayas again!
- Avoid talking about clubbing, socialising with friends, gigs, etc, as this might indicate that you could be unreliable and will roll into work the next day in an unfit state, unable to do your job properly.
- Try not to mention too many interests, as this may give the impression that you will be distracted from doing the job you are applying for. Also, if you are committed to doing evening and weekend work elsewhere, what will happen if there is a deadline to meet at your main place of work and the team needs you to work extra hours in the evening or at a weekend?
- Full reference contact details are not a good idea to include in a CV. Also, applicants sometimes mention their current employer's contact details in their CV. This is not a good idea if your boss does not know that you are looking for a new job! People talk, so it is better to tread with caution.
- 'References are available upon request' is the best way to end a CV. This will also mean that if the names of your contacts change, you will not have to make any amendments to your CV.
- It is always a good idea to keep in touch with the people or person responsible for providing your references so that you are up to speed with their availability should a reference be required quickly.

As mentioned before, check your CV for spelling mistakes. The number of CVs that slip through the net with spelling mistakes can be alarming. Make sure you are not submitting one of those CVs.

Some time ago, CVs were posted or faxed, by either a recruitment agency or the candidate, to a named individual at the company wishing to hire. These days, CVs are often emailed through to a company, or sent via a portal without the name of an individual or HR contact.

A feeling of hopelessness can soon set in if, after a fortnight of waiting for news on job applications you have made, there is no response. It is made more difficult to get an update on an application if you do not have a named hirer to contact directly. This can be one of the downsides if you are searching for a job without the assistance of a recruitment agency. Candidates often choose to register with a recruitment agency when seeking a job, because that way the agency can do the chasing for you.

So, if you decide to look for work without the aid of a recruitment agency and are searching for positions by sourcing opportunities from company websites or job boards, always try and send your CV to a named individual:

- Your details may end up going to many organisations, securely or otherwise, so just to be on the safe side, it will probably be better not to include your full address details, home telephone number, NI number, date of birth, etc, in your CV. Part of your home address (for example, Guildford, Surrey), as well as your email address and mobile telephone number should be enough. Alternatively, you could start by just putting down your email address and mobile number as a point of contact.

- Having said that, if you do include part of your address and you live in Wales but you are applying for a job in, say, Essex, priority might be given to candidates who live in the Essex area, so you could miss out. The hirer may not stop and think that you might also have a legitimate base in Essex; they may presume that moving from Wales to Essex will be a problem for you. In such a case it would be better to just have a mobile contact number and email address in your CV.

- Once you have established a genuine link with the company that is hiring, more personal details can be given. So, remember to hold back in the first instance, just to be on the safe side.

- Most people like children, but you should avoid mentioning them too much in your CV unless you are applying for a job working with children.

- Try and avoid using abbreviations or acronyms in your CV to replace unusual words. However, most people use PR for Public Relations, PA for Personal Assistant, HR for Human Resources, EA for Executive Assistant and CV for Curriculum Vitae; in such instances using acronyms is fine.

- Including a photograph of yourself in your CV is not such a good idea. You may come across as being a little vain.

- Try and avoid having large unexplainable gaps in your CV.

- Also, avoid using too much bold type and too many capital letters. These can be rather hard on the eye.
- Whatever type of job you may be looking for, it is better to keep your CV layout simple, so the right message gets across quickly.
- Avoid using too much creative detail, such as boxes, vibrant colour backdrops, or fancy fonts. Heavy underlining, too many words in bold, capital letters and italics as well as lots of crazy designs are out. If your CV looks a bit like a poster or comic, the hirer will end up getting a headache, become disinterested and then move on to the next CV. Hirers don't like searching for information on a candidate; they like to immediately see and understand what relevant skills a candidate has to offer. Tahoma, Arial or Calibri can be good fonts to use because they look good and are easy to read. You may decide to use font size 11 then drop down to size 10 if you are struggling to get your CV to fit onto two pages.
- If you have been working for many years, it may still be an idea to try and keep your CV down to two pages in length. Although, for example, in the case of a very well-experienced Manager, Director or PA Secretary, three pages can sometimes be acceptable.

Avoid sending your CV out for a job opportunity if you are unable to realistically relocate to where the role is based, if your CV is irrelevant for the role, or if it is any of the following:

- too long
- chaotic in its presentation
- repetitious
- badly typed
- too vague
- too short
- disjointed with dates
- lacking direction
- inconsistent
- out of date
- misleading

Make sure that all the information you provide in your CV is accurate and true. If it is not, the hirer will find out during the interview process and your application will be rejected.

5

The CV suggestions and examples given in this book are there as guidelines. It is up to you to decide how much information you put in your CV.

Basic CV information for an individual with work experience should include:

- name
- email address
- mobile number
- linkedin.com/name (optional)
- profile
- introduction video (optional)
- IT skills
- employment
- training
- education
- achievements
- further information (if applicable)
- interests
- references are available on request
- name and, if you wish, your email address/mobile number at the foot of the second/third page

Basic CV information for a school leaver, college leaver or recent graduate without permanent work experience should include:

- name
- email address
- mobile number
- linkedin.com/name (optional)
- profile
- IT skills
- education
- industrial work placement (if applicable)
- training (if applicable)
- experience (including shop, restaurant, bar work, etc.) while at school and/or university
- achievements (if any)
- interests
- references are available on request

If you need to use a second page, add your name and, if you wish, your email address/mobile number to the foot of that page.

6

Basic CV format

A suggested basic CV format for someone with work experience is given on the next two pages.

Name
(Email address)
Mobile number

Profile:

_____
_____
_____

Employment:

Company Name
Date started to present

Job title
Duties

_____
_____
_____
_____
_____
_____
_____

Company Name
Date started to finish

Job title
Duties

_____
_____
_____
_____
_____
_____
_____

Employment:

Company Name
Date started to finish

Job title
Duties

_____

_____

_____

_____

_____

_____

_____

Training:

_____

IT Skills:

_____

Education & Qualifications:

_____

_____

_____

Achievements:

_____

_____

Interests:

_____

References are available on request

Name
Email

7

If you have held several roles within the same company, it is a good idea not to put each role under a separate heading with the company name repeated each time. If you do you might miss out on being invited for interview because the hirer may get the impression you have had many jobs, that you cannot settle and you will 'continue' to job hop. Please see the section in **Example A** on the following page.

Then please see the section in **Example B** with the changes.

The problem is that most CVs are read 'at a glance'. If the hirer does not see what needs to be seen straightaway, it will be on to the next CV.

Example A

Employment:

A Company Ltd – August 2016 to present
Job title:
Duties

_____

_____

_____

A Company Ltd – August 2015 to July 2016
Job title:
Duties

_____

_____

_____

A Company Ltd – March 2014 to July 2015
Job title:
Duties

_____

_____

_____

B Company Ltd – April 2012 to February 2014
Job title:
Duties

_____

_____

_____

C Company Ltd – January 2010 to March 2012
Job title:
Duties

_____

_____

Please see **Example B**. By presenting the main body of your CV in this way, it is easier to see that you have worked for three different companies while at the same time it is possible to see that you have held five positions. Your CV avoids giving the impression that you have worked for five different companies, and that you have an unsettled work record. As a result, you will stand a greater chance of being selected for interview because it will be easy to spot that your track record is stable.

Example B

Employment:

A Company Ltd – March 2014 to present

Job title (August 2016 to present)
Duties _____
_____
_____

Job title (August 2015 to July 2016)
Duties _____
_____
_____

Job title (March 2014 to July 2015)
Duties _____
_____
_____

B Company Ltd – April 2012 to February 2014

Job title
Duties _____
_____
_____

C Company Ltd – January 2010 to March 2012

Job title
Duties _____
_____
_____

8 School and college leaver CV examples

There now follow suggested ways to present a CV on one page if you are looking for a first job after leaving school or college.

Please see **Examples A, B** and **C.**

Example A

James J
Email: Ja@zmail.com
Mobile: 111 1111

School leaver with retail experience gained in busy, customer-focused environments. I enjoy working within retail sales and would like to secure a permanent shop-based opportunity where I can learn and progress.

IT Skills
Word and Excel

Education

Smithfield School, Clam – September 2012 to July 2019
A Levels:
History (B)
Geography (C)
English (C)

GCSEs:
English (A)
History (A)
Geography (B)
Art (B)
Maths (B)
Science (B)
IT (B)
French (B)

Employment (Part-time while at school)

Clock House Sports Equipment Limited, Clam – September 2018 to July 2019
Sales Assistant
During my time working for this family-owned sports shop, I was responsible for serving customers and giving advice on various sports products and equipment. I dealt with orders and new stock and assisted the manager with cashing up and banking.

Anderson's Supermarket Limited, Clam – January 2018 to August 2018
Cashier
I served customers, used the tills, cashed up and stocked shelves.

Interests
Sport
Computer games
Playing the guitar

References are available on request

Example B

Susan S
Email – s@zmail.com
Mobile – 111 1111

Enthusiastic, hard-working, and organised, I am keen to find an interesting junior secretarial role within a busy and progressive company where I can learn and give support.

Computer Skills
Microsoft, Excel, Outlook

Education

Eastside Tertiary College, Thames Road, Cham – September 2018 to July 2019
Junior Secretarial Course Secretarial & Business Certificate – pass – typing speed 50 wpm
Subjects studied – touch typing, letter writing, email composition, business, and bookkeeping
Other Lawyers, Cham – June 2019
During my secretarial course I spent one week shadowing a Senior Secretary within this firm of solicitors. I was able to learn more about general office procedures such as basic bookkeeping and switchboard duties.

Robin Hood School, Beech Road, Cham – September 2013 to July 2018
GCSEs
English (B) History (B) Geography (C) Art (C) Maths (C) Science (C) IT (C)

Employment (part-time while at college)

Trendy Fashions, Cham – January to May 2019
Sales Assistant
I assisted the manager in this busy boutique. My main duties included:
- Advising and serving customers.
- Ordering of new stock.
- Cashing up and banking.
- Arranging the window display.
- I was also responsible for contacting customers with regards to any new promotions.

Anderson's Supermarkets Ltd, Cham – September to December 2018
Cashier. Duties included:
- Working the tills.
- Serving customers.
- Stocking the shelves.
- Cashing up.

Interests

- Fashion
- Skating
- Reading

References are available on request

Example C

Jessica H
Email – jh@xmail.com
Mobile – 000 0000

I have an outgoing personality and enjoy working with customers. I am keen to work in a creative environment as an administrator/receptionist for either a firm of architects or interior designers.

Education:

Bestway College, Brunton – September 2018 to June 2019
Foundation Diploma in Design
Chalfont School, Brunton – September 2011 to June 2018
A Level: Art B and English D
GCSE: Art, IT, Maths, English, History, Geography, Biology

Computer Skills: Microsoft Office

Employment:

Green Landscape Architects, Brunton – July 2019 to present
Sales Assistant/Administrator
Assist the designers within this busy family business.
- Reception duties
- Process orders
- When customers visit, I direct them to the relevant design manager
- I set up appointments
- Order stock
- Check in deliveries
- Arrange couriers
- Organise lunches

Interests and further information:

Interior Design
Drawing
Painting
Gardening – I am doing a basic course in garden design during my spare time

References are available on request

There now follows a suggested way to present a CV if you are a fresh graduate applying for a post that has nothing to do with the degree gained.

Example **A** without the profile lacks direction.
Example **B** with the profile gives focus to the CV.

Example A

Edgar H
Date of Birth: 1/4/1998
Nationality: British

Home Address
Toad Hall
Bridge Road
Broughton

Mobile: 007 020007
Email: edgarh.com

EDUCATION
2016 – 2019
Anchester University, Somewhere BA English (2:1)

2014 – 2016
Grant High School, Somewhere A-Levels: English, German, Art

2009 – 2014
Grant High School, Somewhere GCSE: Maths, French, German, Chemistry, Biology, Latin, English Language, English Literature, History, Geography, Art, Physics & Drama

WORK EXPERIENCE while at university
Anchester University, Somewhere – 2018 – 2019
Events Coordinator _____
_____
_____
_____

Anchester University, Somewhere – 2017 – 2018
Events Administrator_____
_____
_____
_____

EMPLOYMENT
The Messenger, Hydro – 2015 – 2016
Office Assistant
Supporting the Editor and Journalists _____
_____
_____
_____

Crete Restaurant, Hydro – Summer 2015
Barman
Served drinks to customers and cleared tables_____

_____
_____
_____

ADDITIONAL ACHIEVEMENTS AND SKILLS
IT Skills:
Word, Excel and PowerPoint

Achievements:
Completed the London Marathon 2019
Duke of Edinburgh Award
St John Ambulance First Aid Course
Head Boy

REFERENCE CONTACT DETAILS
Shirley Cluck
Waterways
Arrington

Paul Donald
Vision Zero
13, No Way
Belling

Ms Duck
56, Bakers Dozen
Chamber Lane
Belling

Example B

EDGAR H
Email: edgarh.com
Mob: 007 020007

Motivated and enthusiastic graduate with excellent people skills and the ability to work independently when required. I am determined to secure a progressive role within a successful event company where I can give support. I am a fast learner and an enthusiastic team-player.

IT Skills
Word, Excel, PowerPoint

Education

Anchester University, Somewhere – 2016 to 2019
BA English (2:1)

Grant High School, Somewhere – 2009 to 2016
A-Level: English (B), German (B), Art (D)
GCSE: Maths, French, German, Chemistry, Biology, Latin, English Language, English Literature, History, Geography, Art, Physics & Drama

Employment (part-time while at university)

Anchester University, Somewhere – September 2017 to January 2019
Events Coordinator – February 2018 to January 2019
My duties included_____
_____
_____
_____

Events Administrator – September 2017 to January 2018
My duties included_____
_____
_____
_____

Employment (part-time during sixth form)

The Messenger, Hydro – September 2015 to May 2016
Office Assistant
Supported the Editor and Journalists
Duties included_____
_____
_____
_____

Crete Restaurant, Hydro – July to August 2015
Barman
Duties included_____
_____
_____

Additional Information

Completed the London Marathon 2019
Duke of Edinburgh Award
St John Ambulance First Aid Course
Head Boy

Interests

Tennis
Rugby
Reading
Music
Design

References are available on request

EDGAR H
Email: edgarh.com

Here is a CV comparison for a school leaver.

Example **A** is too fussy.
Example **B** is the suggested correct way because it is easier to read.

Example A

Maggie T
mthorpe.com
Mobile: 077707 00777

Work experience (Saturdays and school holidays part-time):

Time	Company	Position
July 2018–March 2019	*Art Shop Ltd, Hingefield*	*Sales Assistant – served art materials and books to customers. Operated the tills and dealt with refunds.*
November 2017–June 2018	*Jean Shop Ltd, Hingefield*	*Sales Assistant – served customers, cashed up, arranged stock and helped with general duties.*

Education
September 2012–June 2019 St. Hilda's School, Hingefield

A Levels in:
English & Art   A & B Grades

GCSEs in:

Biology	B
Maths	B
French	B
History	B
Chemistry	C
Art	A
Physics	C
English Language	A
English Literature	A

IT Skills – Word, Excel, PowerPoint
Interests – I enjoy Art, Reading, Music, Sport, Baking

Example B

Maggie T
Email: mthorpe.com
Mobile: 077707 00777

I am a quick learner, hard-working and able to follow instructions effectively. I have strong computer skills and work well on my own and as part of a team. I enjoyed English and Art at school. I am passionate about books and am an avid reader. I am very keen to find a junior-level administration role within a publishing company.

IT Skills:
Word,. Excel,. PowerPoint

Education:

St Hilda's School, West Road, Hingefield – September 2012 to June 2019
A Level English (A) and Art (B)
GCSE English Language (A), English Literature (A), Art (A), Biology (B), Maths (B), French (B), History (B), Physics (C) Chemistry (C)

Part-time work experience:

Art Shop Ltd, Hingefield – July 2018 to March 2019
Sales Assistant
Sold art materials and books to customers
Operated the tills and dealt with refunds

Jean Shop Ltd, Hingefield – November 2017 to June 2018
Sales Assistant
Served customers
Cashed up, sorted out stock and assisted with general duties

Interests:

Art
Reading
Music
Sport
Baking

References are available on request

These examples show how to bring the profile on this CV to the point and incorporate the job roles.

Example **A** is too long and repetitious.

Example **B** is the suggested correct way because it is easier to follow and holds the reader's interest.

Example A

George S
10 Upton Street, London SW60
Mobile: 007 0000 000
Email: gsmith.com

Excellent accounts background working in the finance sector as a senior manager. I am good at managing teams and working to very tight deadlines.

Employment
April 2016–March 2019   **Not Limited**
Manager of Finance

_____

_____

_____

_____

_____

_____

January 2015–March 2016   **Not Limited**
Assistant Manager of Finance

_____

_____

_____

_____

_____

_____

September 2013–December 2014   **Not Limited**
Finance Assistant

_____

_____

_____

_____

_____

_____

August 2011–August 2013   **Money Limited**
Administrator

_____

_____

_____

_____

_____

_____

August 2010–August 2011   **PAYE Limited**
Junior Administrator

_____
_____
_____
_____
_____
_____

Education
Ideal University, 2007–2010
BSc (Hons) 2:1 – Business & Finance

Mington Grammar, 2007
A Levels: Law, Business Studies and Maths

Mington Grammar, 2005
GCSEs: Maths, English Language, English Literature, Business Studies,
French, History, Geography, Physics, Chemistry, Biology

Training
Personal development_____
_____

Management training_____
_____

Motivation training_____
_____

Sales skills_____
_____

IT Skills
Word, Excel, PowerPoint, Sage and various packages

Personal
Date of Birth   14th November 1989
Nationality   Swiss
Interests   Reading, cooking, golf, mountaineering and chess

References are available on request

Example B

George S
Email: gsmith.com
Tel: 007 0000 000

Dynamic and successful accounts specialist with an excellent track record of working at senior level within the finance sector. Extremely motivated with strong leadership qualities and the determination to succeed in the most demanding situations. I have led teams of up to 30 staff and thrive when presented with a challenge. I am ambitious and would like to secure a senior management role within a tech finance company.

Employment:

Not Limited, Somewhere – September 2013 to March 2019
Manager of Finance – April 2016 to March 2019

_____
_____
_____
_____

Assistant Manager of Finance – January 2015 to March 2016

_____
_____
_____
_____

Finance Assistant – September 2013 to December 2014

_____
_____
_____
_____

Money Limited, Somewhere – August 2011 to August 2013
Administrator

_____
_____
_____
_____

PAYE Limited, Somewhere – August 2010 to August 2011
Junior Administrator

_____
_____
_____
_____

Education:

Ideal University, Nowhere – 2007 to 2010
BSc (Hons) 2:1 – Business & Finance

Mington Grammar, Mington – 2000 to 2007
A Levels: Law (B), Business Studies (B), Maths (C)
GCSEs: Maths, English Language, English Literature, Business Studies, French, History, Geography, Physics, Chemistry and Biology

Training:

Personal development training_____
_____

Management training_____
_____

Motivation training_____
_____

Sales training_____
_____

IT Skills:

Word, Excel, PowerPoint, Sage, and various bespoke packages

Interests:

Reading, cooking, golf, mountaineering and chess

References are available on request

George S
Email: gsmith.com

Here is how to improve a long and 'unsettled' CV.

In Example **A**, the candidate has not settled into any role and has had too many jobs. There is too much repetition in the profile. Example **B** is shorter, to the point and even though the candidate has moved positions, it is still possible to follow the experience gained without getting bored.

Example A

June M
junem.com

PROFILE
I am an ambitious and motivated person with strong accounting and administration skills. I am a strong team player also able to work as part of a team. I am extremely motivated and can cope remarkably well in highly competitive situations. I have excellent team-building skills and a superb eye for detail. I am keen to find a role within a busy and productive company where my transferable skills can be put into action. I enjoy working towards a goal and will never leave a task incomplete. I am particularly interested in finding an accounts position within a busy department.

KEY SKILLS
Experience using various computer packages including —

EMPLOYMENT HISTORY
Smalls Trading, Longwood – September 2018–March 2019
Financial Assistant (Temporary)
Smalls Trading is a family-run business specialising in food and drink distribution.
My duties included _____

_____

_____

_____

_____

_____

Litts, Longwood – June 2017–August 2018
Financial Assistant (Temporary)
Litts is a printing company offering a full graphics service to the printing industry.
My duties _____

_____

_____

_____

_____

_____

Cushion Covers, Highwood – April–May 2017
Financial Administrator (Temporary)
Cushion Covers is a soft furnishings company supplying to the property development sectors.
My duties _____

_____

_____

_____

_____

_____

Postcard, Highwood – March 2016–March 2017
Financial Administrator (Permanent)
Postcard are a specialist graphics company.
My duties _____

_____

_____

_____

_____

_____

Postcard, Highwood – March 2015–March 2016
Financial Assistant (Permanent)
My duties _____

_____

_____

_____

_____

_____

I also held the following positions:

Financial P/A _____

_____

_____

_____

_____

_____

Financial Secretary _____

_____

_____

_____

_____

_____

Financial Assistant _____

_____

_____

_____

_____

_____

Financial Support _____

_____

_____

_____

_____

_____

Woode Tops, Highwood – January 2015–February 2015
Administration Assistant (Temporary)
Woode Tops is a wood distribution company.
My duties _____

_____

_____

_____

_____

_____

Fos, Highwood – January 2014–December 2014
Finance Assistant (Temporary)
Fos is a camera company.
My duties _____

_____

_____

_____

_____

_____

Has, Highwood – September 2012–December 2013
Finance Administrator (Permanent)
Has is a small family-run engineering firm supplying to the car industry.
My duties were to_____

_____

_____

_____

_____

_____

Media No, Highwood – May 2012–August 2012
Accounts Assistant (Temporary)
Media No is a publishing company.
My duties were to_____

_____

_____

_____

_____

_____

Macede Associates, Highwood – February 2012–April 2012
Accounts Administrator (Temporary)
Macede Associates is a firm of surveyors.
My duties were to_____

_____

_____

_____

_____

_____

Hair Gone Tomorrow, Longwood – July 2007–January 2012
Hairdresser and Beautician (Permanent)
Hair Today is a hair and beauty salon.
My duties were to_____

_____

_____

_____

_____

_____

EDUCATION
Bright College, Leaning – September 2005–July 2007
Hairdressing and Beauty with Finance Diploma
RSA 1 and 2

Bright School, Leaning – 2001–2005
GCSE: English Language B, English Literature B, Maths B, Geography C, Art B, History B

PERSONAL DETAILS
Date of Birth: 8 June 1989
Nationality: British
Address: 61, Nowhere Road, Nowhere
Telephone: Mobile: 0444 121212
Marital Status: Single

Example B

JUNE M
Email: junem.com
Mobile: 0444 121212

Hard-working Accounts Administrator with excellent customer care skills seeks a demanding role as an Accounts Assistant within the financial sector.

EMPLOYMENT:

Smalls Trading, Longwood – September 2018 to March 2019
Smalls Trading is a family-run business specialising in food and drink distribution.
Financial Assistant (Temporary)

_____
_____
_____
_____

Litts, Longwood – June 2017 to August 2018
Litts is a printing company offering a full graphics service to the printing industry.
Financial Assistant (Temporary)

_____
_____
_____
_____

Cushion Covers, Highwood – April to May 2017
Cushion Covers is a soft furnishings company.
Financial Administrator (Temporary)

_____
_____
_____
_____

Postcard, Highwood – March 2015 to March 2017
Postcard is a specialist graphics company.
Permanent roles listed
Financial Administrator

_____
_____
_____
_____

Financial Assistant

_____
_____
_____
_____

Financial P/A

_____
_____
_____
_____

Financial Secretary

_____
_____
_____
_____

Financial Assistant

_____
_____
_____
_____

Financial Support

_____
_____
_____
_____

Woode Tops, Highwood – January to February 2015
Woode Tops is a wood distribution company.
Administration Assistant (Temporary)

_____
_____
_____
_____

Fos, Highwood – January to December 2014
Fos is a camera company.
Finance Assistant (Temporary)

_____
_____
_____

Has, Highwood – September 2012 to December 2013
Has is a small family-run engineering firm that supplies parts to the car industry.
Finance Administrator (Permanent)

_____
_____
_____

Media No, Highwood – May to August 2012
Media No is a publishing company.
Accounts Assistant (Temporary)

_____
_____
_____
_____

Macede Associates, Highwood – February to April 2012
Macede is a firm of surveyors.
Accounts Administrator (Temporary)

_____
_____
_____
_____

Hair Gone Tomorrow, Longwood – July 2007 to January 2012
Hair Today is a hair and beauty salon.
Hairdresser and Beautician (Permanent)

_____
_____
_____
_____

EDUCATION:

Bright College, Leaning – 2005 to 2007
Hairdressing and Beauty with Finance – Diploma
RSA Stages 1 and 2

Bright School, Leaning – 2001 to 2005
GCSE: English Language B, English Literature B, Mathematics B, Geography C, Art B, History B

IT SKILLS:

Word, Excel, Sage

INTERESTS:

Cooking, Fashion, Beauty

References are available on request.

June M
Mobile: 0444 121212

Example A shows a CV for a graduate with limited work experience since graduation. The positioning of the industrial work placement experience gives the CV more substance.

Example A

ANTONIA B
email – ablat.co.uk
mobile – 08777 9000

Marketing graduate with agency and industry experience keen to secure a challenging and demanding Account Executive role within a dynamic and successful integrated marketing agency.

EMPLOYMENT:

No Such Agency, Somewhere – September 2018 to present
Junior Account Executive
Working on client accounts for Spence and Mark, Habit, Nest and Hand
My duties include:
*   Attending meetings with clients and suppliers
*   Giving full support to the Account Managers and Directors
*   Writing briefs and _____
*   Contacting the creative teams for_____
*   Being responsible for full feedback to_____
*   _____
*   _____
*   _____
*   _____
*   _____
*   _____

Any Company, Somewhere – September 2016 to September 2017 (industrial work placement)
Marketing Executive
As part of my degree I worked for this fashion house.
Any Company specialise in the design and distribution of _____
I was responsible for the following:
*   Assisted the Marketing Manager with the promotion of _____
*   _____
*   _____
*   _____
*   _____
*   _____
*   _____
*   _____
*   _____
*   _____

EMPLOYMENT (while at school and university):

J & K Shops Ltd, Somewhere – January 2015 to August 2016
Shop Assistant
My job involved serving customers, cashing up and ordering stock as well as_____

* _____
* _____
* _____
* _____
* _____

Smith Ltd, Somewhere – April 2012 to December 2014
Waitress
Duties included serving customers, taking in stock_____

* _____
* _____
* _____
* _____
* _____

EDUCATION:

Oldcastle University, Nowhere – 2014 to 2018
BA (Hons) 2:1 in Marketing
Modules included International Marketing, Business Marketing and Advertising

Greys School, Somewhere – 2007 to 2014
A level: English A, Biology A and Business Studies A
GCSE: Mathematics, History, Geography, Physics, English Language, English Literature, Religious Education and Art

IT SKILLS:

Word, Excel

INTERESTS:

Reading, Sport, Design

References are available on request

Antonia B
email – ablat.co.uk

Examples A, **B** and **C** are three further example CVs of candidates who have more work experience.

Example A

Chris J
email – cjme@snail.com
mobile – 07770 600000 – linkedin.com/name

I am a highly adaptable and experienced Account Handler with a broad range of skills
gained _____

_____

_____

_____

*Click * for my brief introduction video.*

IT SKILLS
Microsoft Office – Word, Excel, PowerPoint

EMPLOYMENT

No Communications, Marketing Agency, Nowhere – November 2018 to present
Account Handler
I worked closely with the Senior Account Director on the following accounts:

- _____
- _____
- _____
- _____
- _____
- _____

Get Off, Marketing Agency, Nowhere – May to November 2018
Office Administrator
Reported to the Marketing Director

- _____
- _____
- _____
- _____
- _____
- _____

How Design, Nowhere – April 2017 to May 2018
Accounts Assistant
Reported to the Accounts Director

- _____
- _____
- _____
- _____
- _____
- _____

Masda Supermarkets, Nowhere – May 2014 to March 2017
Administrator (Part-time then full time after college) – November 2014 to March 2017

- _____
- _____
- _____
- _____
- _____
- _____

Retail Assistant (Part-time) – May 2014 to October 2014

- _____
- _____
- _____
- _____
- _____
- _____

EDUCATION

No Such College, Some Town – 2013 to 2015
HND Design Communications
Modules included

_____
_____

Buckingham Street High School, Some Town – 2006 to 2013
A Level History A, Biology A, Art C
GCSEs in 10 subjects including English and Mathematics

FURTHER TRAINING

First Aid Course 2015
PADI Qualified Open Water Diving Certificate

INTERESTS

Sport, Fishing, Cooking, Museums and Chess

References are available on request

Chris J
email – cjme@snail.com

Example B

Beta C
Email – bc@.qom
Mobile – 07777 88833 – linkedin.com/beta

Dedicated, motivated and innovative Marketing Manager with extensive experience of promoting and improving the performance of a broad range of brands. Effective worker with excellent leadership qualities, I thrive on responsibility and am highly adaptable and professional with a flexible, determined approach. My focus is to secure a senior managerial role within a creative, forward-thinking organisation.

Employment

Another Design Company, Nowhere – August 2012 to present
Marketing Manager: April 2017 to present
Senior Executive: August 2015 – March 2017
Marketing Executive: August 2012 – July 2015

I was promoted from the position of Marketing Executive to the position of **Marketing Manager** reporting directly to the Marketing Director.
- **Managing all areas of the marketing** for this awarding-winning design company:
  _____
  _____
  _____
  _____
  _____
  _____

- **Marketing materials**_____
  _____
  _____
  _____

- **Events**_____
  _____
  _____
  _____

- **PR**_____
  _____
  _____
  _____

Notable Achievements
  _____
  _____
  _____
  _____
  _____
  _____

A Another Agency, Nowhere – July 2009 to September 2009 (Work Experience)
Marketing Executive
- Worked for the Marketing Department _____
  _____
  _____
  _____
  _____

B Another Agency, Nowhere – June 2009 (Work Experience)
Marketing Assistant
- Worked in the Communications Department_____
  _____
  _____
  _____
  _____

C Another Agency, Nowhere – May 2009 (Work Experience)
Marketing Intern
- Assisted the consumer team_____
  _____
  _____
  _____
  _____

IT Skills & Training

InDesign, Photoshop, Microsoft Word, Outlook, Excel, Illustrator
Social Media tools – Facebook Ad Manager and analytics
CIM Professional Certificate in Marketing
Project Management Course
Media Training

Education

Forde University, Nowhere – 2009 to 2012
English Literature and Language BA (Hons) 2:1 Hons
Ridge College, Nowhere – 2007 to 2009
3 A Levels – Art B, History C, Design Technology C
Ridge School, Nowhere – 2002 to 2007
10 GCSEs

Achievements & Interests

Duke of Edinburgh Award
Voluntary work in Columbia for an orphanage
Fundraiser for Cancer Research – Running Race for Life each year since 2016
Music, Yoga, Reading, Design, Ballet, Charity Work, Keeping Fit

References are available on request

Beta C
bc@.qom

Example C

Caroline T
email ct@not.com
06700 111111

Dedicated and reliable PA with a solid track record of giving supreme support to Senior Directors. I am methodical and can work to deadlines with ease and in a professional manner gaining maximum results. I have successfully liaised with clients at all levels and can prioritise workloads effectively and with the minimum of fuss. Currently seeking a demanding and rewarding PA role.

SKILLS:

- Proficient and fluent use of Microsoft Office
- Sage
- Confident using cloud and Social Media technologies
- Audio typing – 60wpm
- Minute taking
- Shorthand – 100wpm

EMPLOYMENT HISTORY:

Financial, Nowhere Town – May 2016 to March 2020
EA to the Chief Executive Officer
Duties

- _____

- _____

- _____

- _____

- _____

- _____

- _____

- _____

- _____

- _____

Mo UK, Nowhere Town – January 2013 to April 2016
PA to the Director of Operations
Duties

* _____
  _____
* _____
  _____
* _____
  _____
* _____
  _____
* _____
  _____
* _____
  _____
* _____
  _____
* _____
  _____
* _____
  _____

Me UK, Nowhere Town – July 2011 to January 2013
PA to the Finance Director
Duties

* _____
  _____
* _____
  _____
* _____
  _____
* _____
  _____
* _____
  _____
* _____
  _____
* _____
  _____
* _____
  _____

Caroline T
email ct@not.com
mobile 06700 111111

HNWI, Nowhere Town – July 2009 to June 2011
Private Family PA
Duties

- _____
  _____
- _____
  _____
- _____
  _____
- _____
  _____
- _____
  _____
- _____
  _____
- _____
  _____
- _____
  _____
- _____
  _____

EDUCATION:

Loads Secretarial College, Somewhere – 2008 to 2009
RSA 1 and 11 Distinction
Shorthand – 90wpm
Word, Excel, Outlook

Grind University, Nowhere – 2005 to 2008
BSc 2:1 (Hons) Geography

Easy School, Somewhere – 1998 to 2005
9 GCSEs & 3 A-Levels

INTERESTS:

Theatre, Politics, Tennis, Design, Photography

REFERENCES ARE AVAILABLE ON REQUEST

Caroline T
email ct@not.com
mobile 06700 111111

10 Deciding on the best sort of position

Ideally you should look for a job that will suit your experience and personality. Perhaps you have just left school or college; you may be returning to the job market after having children; or you could be a more mature candidate wishing to return to work because your children have grown up and left home.

It is important to know what sort of company you may wish to work for, and you should also have a general idea of the sort of job role you are seeking.

You might need to show you have transferable skills, so it is better not to be too rigid with your requirements.

Most companies require employees to have an ability to be 'several departments rolled into one'. During an interview, hirers will expect interviewees to demonstrate that they are helpful, flexible multitaskers.

This expectation will also apply to candidates looking for roles in the secretarial sector. PAs and Executive Assistants will certainly need to show they can be adaptable. The days of demanding a high salary and expecting to sit at your desk outside the boss's office ready to carry out only superior duties specifically for your boss are over. Everyone, regardless of level, will be required to help with whatever tasks need to be completed.

It is vital to demonstrate during an interview, that you have the right attitude if you want to get the job you are applying for.

Candidates sometimes lack confidence in finding new employment once they are over a certain age. The breakdown of work experience outlined in a CV will give an indication that you may be someone of more mature years: there is no easy way to disguise your age.

It is important to work in an environment that relishes the experience of a more mature individual. Show the correct levels of enthusiasm and you will secure the right position. It may also help if you are flexible when it comes to the type of job you are seeking. Choose a company that will value your experience and input; there are many such organisations around. If you are well presented and have a good personality, there is every chance you will secure a rewarding role, irrespective of your age.

The best thing to do is offer a full CV detailing your experience, but as mentioned before, two rather than three pages will be a more attractive option.

So, you are still single and hurtling towards being north of thirty, or older. You might therefore be keen to look for a new job and a rich partner! For this reason, you may decide to use your attributes by firstly presenting a photograph of yourself on the first page of your CV, then if you secure an interview you may eye up your very attractive interviewer, who could potentially be, or become, your boss.

Big rule – avoid making every effort to get a job specifically because you fancy the person who potentially could be your boss. Yes, some bosses might be open to having an affair, but once the affair is over you may also find that you are out of a job.

Whether your potential boss looks like Quasimodo or George Clooney, Angelina Jolie, or a pantomime dame, take the job because you really want to do the job, not because you like the look of the person who could be your boss.

If you are 35 plus, without children and newly married, you may find that job offers do not necessarily come your way easily. A prospective employer could be concerned that you might want to start a family soon after joining the company. The interviewer will not be able to ask, but it can be a concern to some hirers because of the struggle to find suitable fill-in staff. It will be up to you to work hard at convincing the interviewer that you are the right person for the position because of your knowledge and experience.

If you are a parent coping with children, the pressures of full-time work may not be for you. Parents sometimes feel that they are ready to return to employment when their child reaches school age. The parent may feel able to work a full day because the child will be collected from school by a friend or family member when school finishes. What happens if your child becomes unwell? The answer is often, 'My child is never unwell.'

It is not a good idea to rely totally on using schools as a babysitting service. If long hours of work are required (they often are), and deadlines need to be met, there may be a lot of pressure on you to perform your duties in the workplace, or from home. That, coupled with the pressures home life can often present, might mean it may not be possible to do a demanding job effectively.

Your contract of employment may say that the hours of work are 9am to 5.30pm, but in fact, you could be expected to work from 8.30am till 6pm and beyond. On top of this, working from a laptop once home in the evening is not uncommon. So, if you think taking a laptop home is an easy way of doing those extra hours out of the office, you may need to think again, especially if you have children at home who need attention. Thanks to video conferencing tools, we are all expected to be available to complete a longer, more flexible working day, whether we like it or not!

Political correctness prevents the interviewer from asking the interviewee sensible and realistic questions. By avoiding certain topics during an interview, it may seem easier to secure a position, but is it going to be possible to hold down the post successfully in the long term?

Most people need to work for financial reasons. So, if you have young children and you are looking to secure a position, make sure it is a role you can realistically do so that your children don't suffer and your work colleagues don't feel that you are not pulling your weight.

It is better to take on a position that will provide you with the support you need when you need it, a job you know you can do. When you have young children, applying for part-time work can often be the answer.

This will make it possible to talk about home commitments without feeling uncomfortable. If you are lucky enough to have good backup from family members, or a couple of close friends, it may help to mention this during an interview if the need to discuss childcare arrangements arises.

Any company you apply to for a home-based role, will still invite you to their offices for an interview if they are interested in taking your application further. When this happens, be prepared to follow the rules and have your interview techniques up to date, as the company will want to see that you have the ability to represent them in the correct manner if you get the job.

If you have been out of the loop for a while, it is important to know that even the most informal interview should be taken seriously, especially if the hirer suggests you go in for an informal chat.

A prospective employer will look at you as 'a package', therefore you might need to think to yourself, 'Does my application tick all of the boxes?' You may miss out to another candidate for the most basic reason. The simplest things can often determine whether you get the job.

For example:

- Do you live near to the place of work?
- Is your journey to work easy?
- Do you drive and have a car?
- Will your journey to work be easy during the winter months?
- If the bus and train service is infrequent, how would you get to work?

It is always worth checking the location of any company you are applying to just in case there is no public transport nearby. It may be necessary to drive and have a car because some organisations are situated in the most difficult of places to access.

Commitments outside the workplace can be a problem to those inside the workplace:

- Are you studying a course at college in the evenings that is relevant to your work? If so, how easy would it be for you to get to your course on time?
- Would your childcare arrangements mean you would need to leave the workplace at a set time?
- How would you handle staying late to do work?

It is good to know how to deal with any questions that may relate to working extra hours at the beginning or end of the day.

The job market is competitive and going for interviews is costly. So, while you may easily secure an interview, make sure you have a good chance of getting the role. Try not to take on an interview for a role that is more than you can realistically manage.

Questions you may like to ask yourself that could help you decide what sort of job role to go for:

- Why do you need to work?
- Do any of your friends have just the job you would like?
- What are you looking for in your new job?
- Who do you admire the most in the workplace and why?
- Which well-known person do you admire?

If you are struggling to find the right sort of job in a competitive job market and are desperate to start earning, it might be an idea to revisit how you are going about your job search so the best outcome can be achieved. The obvious next step might be to apply for a basic sort of job that may not stretch you as much as you would like. If you are offered such a role, you could take it then create an interest in your spare time that could give you the right balance while earning. Or you could enrol to do an evening course. Perhaps it will be easier to decide what to do if you assess:

- How relevant your qualifications are to the jobs that you are applying for?
- What course you would like to do in your spare time?
- What interests could you take up to compensate for lack of job satisfaction?

For school leavers, college leavers or graduates:

- Would you study the same course or degree again if you had the chance to revisit your choices?

If the answer is Yes and the jobs you are applying for match what you have studied, then fine.

If your answer is No then perhaps pursuing an outside interest or course that matches what you wish you had studied could compensate for the lack of genuine passion you may have for the jobs you are to apply for.

- If you had your time again what would you have studied/chosen to do for a living? For example, would you have trained to become a doctor, a hairdresser, a lawyer, a fashion designer, an architect, a secretary, a nurse, or anything else?

There are so many courses you can do during your spare time. So, whatever job you decide to go for, the best way to stay positive and get the best out of a job you may not have set your heart on will be to do a course you are passionate about. Nowadays, if you are lucky enough to get the 'perfect' job that suits your needs, then great. But given how competitive the job market is, it may be necessary to settle into a job you are not so passionate about so you can get a steady salary. Just as long as the people you could be working with are nice, be enthusiastic and take the job you are offered and balance your other needs via a course on a subject you are passionate about that doesn't interfere with any aspect of your working day.

Whatever job you are applying for, if you are invited for an interview, make sure you are well prepared when you attend and do everything you can to get that job.

11 Personal presentation

An interview costs time and money, so you need to get your presentation right first time.

The more traditional way of dress will be necessary when it comes to how you present yourself for an interview. This will certainly apply if you are interviewing for more conventional, office-based roles.

Getting the balance right can be difficult sometimes: you don't want to attend an interview dressed as though you are going to a wedding, a party, or a funeral.

Most people dress casually for work, but it is important not to dress casually for an interview, no matter what the industry.

The dressing-down culture will need to stop if you want to get that job.

The following are out if you are looking for a job in a progressive sort of organisation:

- **Low-slung, frayed/ripped jeans with pants, thongs or boxers showing**. You may be applying for a position with a creative agency where you think this look is acceptable, but duties in the role may include attending meetings with agency clients that could range from event organisations to firms of solicitors. So, even though the dress code within a creative agency environment may be very casual, you should avoid adopting the relaxed look at an interview. Those conducting the interview need to feel confident that you can also look smart should it be necessary to involve you in meetings with clients, corporate or otherwise.
- **Designer clothing with a creased finish**. This look can be misunderstood. The label may be high-end but if you wear such clothing in the wrong environment, such as the workplace, you may end up presenting yourself in an unprofessional way. Save your creased designer clothing for a night out clubbing.

- **Creased shirt or blouse**. If you decide to wear a creased shirt or blouse under your jacket that shows, there is every likelihood that you will not be invited back for a second interview. Badly creased clothes that are supposed to be ironed indicate a slovenly attitude.

- **Boots, long or short, worn with a skirt or with trousers**. It will not matter how good the cut of the skirt or the trousers, or how expensive the boots. The look will be mismatched and too casual for an interview.

- **Bare legs**. If you wear a skirt, or trousers and have bare legs, this will show a lack of effort and can make your presentation look very down-market.

- **Short skirts**. This look is not at all suitable for an interview, and you will not be taken seriously.

- **Tight skirts or trousers**. These do not look at all smart on anyone; best to avoid showing a visible panty line or any other sort of underwear line!

- **Sandals**. It does not matter how nicely polished your toenails are, or whether your sandals are Jimmy Choo, sandals are out.

- **High-heeled shoes, stilettos, platforms**. Not smart enough. Also, you may fall over.

- **Multiple earrings, studs and/or rings**. No, take them off or out. One pair will be fine, and they should not be big. Wear multiple earrings for your interview, then afterwards sit and wonder why you did not get the job. If you are going for a job behind a bar then fine, maybe! But that look is unsuitable for most office environments.

- **Wacky hair colours**. Even subtle two-tones are a no.

- **Tongue and facial piercings**. This is a difficult one. I suppose if you have a leaning towards having such decorative pieces, the likelihood is that you will not be applying for an office job. If you do decide to put yourself forward for an office role, they will need to be removed.

- **Tattoos**. Loads of people have 'tatts' these days, but for an interview they are best kept hidden under clothing, if possible. If your tattoos are on your hands, or up your neck or on your face, and you regret having them there, perhaps they could be removed, especially if you want your job applications to be taken seriously. If you choose to keep them very visible, it may mean that the sort of jobs you are applying for will not be based in either a traditional office environment or a high-end creative environment.

- **The 'unkempt hair look'**. Perhaps in moderation, but a lot will depend upon your age and the culture of the company that is hiring. Having said that, a certain Prime Minister, old enough to know better, took it upon himself to adopt this look – he may have secured his position while sporting such a messy hairstyle, but you will be taking a risk if you choose to wear your hair in such an untidy way for an interview. With a more moderate version of this style you may pass the dress code, but you could be pushing your luck and therefore miss out on the offer of a job if your hair looks untidy. By opting for a neat haircut, you will make a much better impression when attending face-to-face interviews and video interviews. A hirer will take your job application more seriously too.
- **Stubble**. This may be the look of movie stars and footballers, but, if you are going for interviews, you will need to make the effort beforehand and have a proper shave. Why look as though you have spent a night or two out on the tiles and jeopardise the opportunity of getting a job, especially one you may really want?
- **Beards**. These are best kept short and neat.
- **Roots**. If you dye your hair make sure your natural roots are not showing, as this look will ruin any smart appearance you may wish to achieve. So, book an appointment with your hairdresser, and get your roots done before your interview.
- **Cleavage on display**. What on earth are you trying to achieve? That look will send out all the wrong signals and you will not get the job.
- **Leather**. Far too casual.
- **Heavily patterned suit**. Too theatrical.
- **Back seamed tights, or stockings**. Not the right image.
- **Cardigan**. All too homely. No matter how expensive the cardigan, it just is not going to be smart enough.
- **Perfume or aftershave**. Best not to apply either.

When it comes to what to wear for an interview, you may choose to follow these suggestions:

- If possible, invest in a tailored, long-sleeved skirt suit/trouser suit, or suit. It might be an idea to choose a safe colour such as dark grey, navy, or black. Team the suit with a smart blouse or a white shirt with a collar that is the right fit and a plain, nondescript tie (avoid heavy patterns).

- Discreet cufflinks.
- Avoid wearing a jacket, or trousers in a bright colour.
- If you are wearing a skirt, the length should ideally be to on the knee, certainly no shorter.
- Wear natural colour stockings/tights, even during warm weather.
- Wear polished classic plain black or navy court shoes with a heel of not much more than two inches. Or smart, classic-style black or dark brown lace-ups.
- Carry a standard-size bag, whatever your preference, ideally the same colour as your shoes.
- Wear a limited amount of plain jewellery.
- Don't wear heavy makeup, especially if you are having a video interview.
- Have neatly cut, styled hair.
- Keep your nails clean and tidy.
- Acrylic hard gel and nail extensions should look as natural as possible, so no jazzy colours when it comes to nail polish. If you decide to wear nail polish, best choose a natural colour.
- Carry a neat folder or portfolio.
- Make sure you take an ironed handkerchief or tissues just in case you need to unexpectedly wipe your nose!
- Take your own pen.
- Wear an overcoat, if applicable.
- Carry a small umbrella (nothing looks worse than turning up for an interview looking like a drowned rat).

It is a good idea to check and, if necessary, iron your interview outfit a few days before your interview. If your outfit has not been worn for some time, give it an airing to get rid of any musty smells.

If you are an older candidate on interview, try and present yourself in a way that suits your age. The opportunity to get a job may go against you if you dress too young; it is important not to look frumpy either because that never goes down well, so try and get the balance right. Even though the pressure is for you to look eternally youthful, there are dress codes for all ages. Every decade you clock up requires a presentation adjustment. So, just be yourself and look smart.

12 Personal hygiene

This can be bit of a difficult subject to talk about, but it does need to be dealt with.

Most candidates do not have a problem with personal hygiene, but a small number do. Nerves can make a person sweat more than usual; it might be a hot day and the candidate has rushed to the interview, or the interview room may be warm on a cold day.

Whatever the circumstances, make sure you prevent an unexpected sweat rush from happening by applying a generous amount of deodorant and, if possible, make sure the fabric next to your skin is made of natural fibres so that your body gets some sort of ventilation. There are plenty of ways to avoid body odour becoming an issue, so make sure you do what is necessary. If you smell, you will not get the job.

Surprisingly, many people attending interviews also suffer from bad breath. Try using a suitable mouthwash if you know you suffer from this problem.

- It really is best not to eat spicy food the night before your interview. Apart from the fact that it could upset your stomach causing you to miss the interview altogether, how do you think garlic and onion 'fumes' will be welcomed during your interview the next day?
- Cigarette breath can be equally off-putting. Just a couple of puffs on a fag before your interview, that is all you need to do to create offensive breath. It is best not to have a cigarette before your appointment. If you must smoke, remember to use a breath freshener immediately afterwards.
- Never chew gum during an interview.
- If you have bad breath because of dental problems, it is important to see your dentist and get the problem sorted out quickly. Some people have a problem with bad breath because they do not eat properly.
- Try not to drink alcohol the night before your interview. Apart from the fact that you will not want to have a hangover on the day of your

interview, alcohol breath can be just about the worst smell to give off at an interview. It will also give off a worrying message about you.

- Tea or coffee on an empty stomach can also make the breath smell unpleasant, so stick to water.
- If you have an interview in the morning, eat breakfast beforehand and keep a packet of extra-strong mints in your pocket so you can freshen up with one just before your interview.

An interview costs time and money. If you choose to ignore these basic guidelines, you will be wasting your time and money because you will not get the job; it will go to someone else who is better prepared.

13 Communicate

The pressure of job hunting can create huge emotional tensions all around. So, spare a few minutes to think about those closest to you when you are looking for a job.

Some people say that they get excited about looking for a job, but your enthusiasm may not stretch that far. If instead you are nervous, try sharing how your job search is making you feel with someone close; this may help you change your perspective and relieve you of any stress and anxiety.

Perhaps you could involve a member of your family, a partner or close friend when it comes to the preparations you are making for your job hunt. Sometimes, useful comments can come from the most unlikely quarters. It is a good idea to get feedback as you go through the various stages of compiling your CV. Perhaps discuss your planned interview techniques, roleplay if possible. Ask for an opinion about your interview outfit and how you plan to present yourself so you can be sure you are doing things correctly.

Try and view your search for a job as a project, so the whole experience does not seem like too much of a chore.

14   Time keeping

It is important to always be on time for an interview. If you are late, it will not matter how well you perform, the chances of you being offered the job will be greatly reduced:

- Always check where the company is situated well before your interview. If possible, visit the location beforehand.
- Avoid telephoning the company where your interview is being held to ask whether you can use their staff car park.
- Arriving with ten minutes to spare before the interview, may not allow you enough time to compose yourself, or reach the right part of the building where the interview is taking place.
- If you plan to travel by car, make sure you allow plenty of time to find a bay and pay, if that is the only method of parking available. Where possible, use a car park or a free parking area. That way you will be able to relax during your interview because there will be no time constraints to distract you. An interview can sometimes last for quite a while, especially if it is going well. You would not want to cut your appointment short due to parking issues, because that would make you look disinterested and unprofessional.
- When going for an interview, it is best not to park in the staff car park, because you would not want to draw attention to yourself if your car was to get blocked in. A parking problem could result after your interview, which would be most embarrassing for you.
- If you are catching a train, make sure you allow at least an hour extra for your journey, to cover cancellations. Delays due to rail work or bad weather can often occur inside and outside the rush-hour period.
- The same extra journey time rule should apply if you are travelling by car. School runs starting from the middle of the afternoon often cause huge traffic problems.

- If your interview is being held in a large office building, you will need to leave plenty of time to get through security. If you are 20 minutes early, this will be an acceptable time to arrive at reception, ready and composed for your interview. It is worth remembering that you may need to sign in with reception and be given a visitor badge to wear. All this could take extra time, especially if there is a queue.

- It is an obvious thing to mention, but always make sure you have enough fuel in your vehicle before setting off. It pays to give yourself plenty of time for your journey so that if you have a problem, for example a puncture or flat battery, you will have the chance to get a taxi.

15   How to stay calm before and during an interview

This is always going to be a difficult one. Some people never get nervous during interviews and some people go to pieces. We can be our own worst enemy when it comes to nerves before an interview.

Some guidelines to help calm your nerves:

- Research the company well in advance of the interview.
- Don't start doing your research the night before your interview if you want to avoid developing last-minute nerves.
- Make a few notes that you can refer to for final preparation well before your interview.
- Try not to take pages of notes with you to the interview as it can be easy to get into a muddle when referring to them.
- Avoid presenting a copy of your CV at an interview unless you are told to do so.
- Make sure your portfolio is in order if you are taking one.
- Avoid getting your hair done on the day of your interview.
- Arrive in plenty of time.
- It is best not to attend an interview laden with luggage or carrier bags. When entering a situation where you are likely to be nervous, the less there is to carry the better. Also, you do not want to give the impression you are clumsy or forgetful by dropping things or leaving anything behind.
- If you plan to wear comfy shoes to get to the interview, then change into smart shoes for the actual interview; do not change into them in reception! Find somewhere discreet away from the building where you are being interviewed. The same applies when your interview finishes, and you are ready to leave; do not change back into comfy shoes in reception!
- Avoid having a cigarette outside the building where the interview will

be held. Remember, there is likely to be CCTV at the main entrance and within the immediate vicinity.

- As mentioned before, visit the company's location a day or two before the interview if you can.
- Take a lucky item that is small and can be kept in your pocket.
- Remember to turn off your mobile phone well before your interview.
- Be enthusiastic about your interview.

If you follow the guidelines and have tried your best at job interviews, but were unsuccessful each time, make sure you get feedback. You'll then avoid making the same mistakes during any future interviews, and you will be reassured that you completed all your preparations to the best of your ability and are in better shape next time to get that job.

A third of your time can be spent in the workplace, so when you attend an interview it is important to feel comfortable with the job, the location, the surroundings, and the people.

Always try and have your interviews during peak office hours; that way you will be able to get an impression of the working environment. Hopefully, reception will make you feel at ease and you will be able to observe quite a lot from your seat in the reception area while you wait to be called in for your interview.

If, say, after the second or third interview stage, you are invited out for lunch as a formality by your prospective boss or company, avoid drinking any alcohol, even if it is offered to you. You may relax too much, end up saying the wrong things and miss out on a definite offer.

Remember, even at this late stage, the final decision could be between you and someone else, so it is important to stay calm, and on guard all the way through the interview process, even if it takes place in informal surroundings.

16 What to say during an interview and how to project your personality

The aim of the interviewer is to fill the role with the ideal candidate at the earliest possible opportunity.

The aim of the interviewee is to get the ideal role at the earliest possible opportunity.

Preparation is key, so:

- Make sure you have studied the job description fully before your interview.
- Base your prepared questions on what you have read from the job description, the company's website, the internet, and company brochure, if they have one.
- If you feel nervous, ask yourself why?

Make every effort not to feel nervous, because the more often you do, the more times you will have to go through the interview process. Why give the job opportunity to someone else because you have allowed your nerves to ruin your interview technique?

- Always maintain good eye contact with the person interviewing you.
- Good deportment is important if you want to make the right impression.
- How you carry yourself will be noticed when you are being greeted.
- No slouching or hands in pockets.

Some people think handshaking is old-fashioned, but it is not. Usually, in an interview, a good firm handshake is vital when you first meet the person or people who will conduct your interview. It is also usual to remember the handshake at the end of the interview too. Handshaking actions will of course depend on any current health situations. So, unless there is a viable excuse not to handshake, for example if there is a cold or serious virus going around, and an alternative way of greeting is introduced, the following should apply:

- When meeting for the first time, it is important to be polite and professional by offering a handshake. Handshakes can tell a lot about strength of character too.
- When you get to your interview do not go over the top by giving a knuckle-cruncher handshake; a short, firm handshake will suffice. Practise on your friends or a member of your family so you get the grip right.
- There can be nothing worse than giving or receiving a limp, damp handshake. If you suffer from sweaty palms due to nerves, dry them discreetly, and I mean discreetly, on something such as a handkerchief. Do not let the interviewer catch you wiping your hand on your trousers or skirt!
- Give a firm handshake with good eye contact and a friendly smile.
- Sit upright during the interview. Junior candidates should avoid adopting a vulture-like sitting position, so make sure your posture is in check.
- If you slouch you will give the impression that you are not at all interested in the role that is being discussed, or anything else for that matter.
- The ideal interview scenario will be if your interview is one-to-one. However, if you are faced with a panel interview, do not be put off. Remain composed, give good eye contact, and answer all the questions you are asked clearly and concisely.

Examples of possible questions that a less experienced candidate may be asked:

- Question: Why do you want a job, for example in marketing?
- Answer: Because I studied marketing at university and completed a year in industry with Fragrances Limited, a cosmetic company. I held the position of Marketing Assistant and my duties included...

Good continuation between interviewer and interviewee.

- Question: Why do you want a job in marketing?
- Answer: Because I studied history at university.
- Question: What has history got to do with marketing?
- Answer: Erm... I don't know!

> *Due to lack of preparation you may have ended the interview without meaning to. A better response would have been to have spoken about any research into marketing you might have done to support your interest and show your determination to get into the sector.*

- Question: Why do you want a job in marketing?
- Answer: Because after college I worked as a temporary administrator for various companies. I then found a temporary reception/administration role with a marketing agency which I really enjoyed. I now realise that marketing is the career path I wish to follow. I will be enrolling to study a marketing course during my spare time.

> *Good continuation between interviewer and interviewee.*

Knowing about a relevant course will help create a better conversation between you and the interviewer, which will give your interview more of an edge.

No matter how confident you may be, nerves can sometimes play havoc, especially when you are trying to make the right impression. It is important for the interviewee to remember that the interviewer can also be just as nervous, so a little light-hearted conversation can hold the interview together and prevent pregnant pauses. This is where talking about hobbies and interests can sometimes 'break the ice' for all concerned. Allow the interviewer to bring up the topic of hobbies and interests.

If you are feeling nervous, hopefully the interviewer will pick this up from you quickly and put you at ease. However, a lot may depend upon how much the interviewer wants, or is able, to make you feel relaxed. Sometimes, if you tell the interviewer you feel nervous, a short conversation may be created on that very subject and before you know it you will feel fine. But as I mentioned, this will depend upon the person who is interviewing you.

If you happen to feel relaxed anyway, do not fall into the trap of being too familiar by talking a lot and going off on tangents, telling jokes or laughing too much; that will lose you the job. Just carry on asking and answering questions in a professional, yet friendly way. Remember to listen:

- Always ask questions at an interview.
- Make sure the questions you ask are well thought through.
- Even if you think you may know the answer to the most obvious questions, it still pays to ask. This will show that you are interested.
- Try and plan what questions you may wish to ask well before the interview.

If during the interview you are asked what your ambitions are, give an answer that directly fits the role you are applying for:

- You could say that you are keen to settle into the position and grow with the company. Explain why by giving relevant examples.
- If you come across as being overambitious, you may give the impression that you will not settle into the role.
- It is important to be enthusiastic about career progression; go easy though or you may not be called for a second or third interview.
- Always let the interviewer lead. Avoid trying to take over the interview and don't pre-empt any of the questions.

How to deal with the strength and weakness question.

- Try and focus on your good points. Avoid giving specific negative points such as bad time keeping, impatience, preference to working alone.
- Instead, perhaps turn one of your strengths into a weakness, for example, you could say you find it difficult to leave a task until it has been completed, or that you are an early riser and are often the first one to arrive at work. Stop short so you don't sound like a workaholic!
- Give examples to explain how well you have worked under pressure and to strict deadlines. Perhaps mention teamwork and your willingness to work extra hours to get the job done. Talk briefly about some completed projects where your input has been key.

Some organisations do not always indicate that they are likely to test the candidate:

- Be prepared for any unexpected test situations.
- You may be asked to do a competency-based test online.
- You may be asked to complete an IT test.
- Take your favourite pen, because you may need to complete a written test or fill out some details.

Sometimes prospective employers want to see that you have neat and legible handwriting. Handwriting can say a lot about a person.

If you are going for an interview with a large company, it is highly likely you will be tested. Some tests may be time limited. It is important to find out as much as you can about the format of any test either via your recruitment consultant, if you have one, the HR contact or hirer at the company, well before your interview so you can prepare.

Answer the question with an answer:

- Try to create a short conversation around your answers but avoid rambling on.
- Candidates have often lost out on job roles because of too much talking.
- Don't read from your CV. This could look as though you don't know much about yourself, or that you may not be telling the truth about your application.
- It is best not to produce notepads, pens, or other items when first arriving for an interview. If you want to take notes, it might be an idea to ask first. You may even find that it is not necessary to take notes at all.

> During each interview, it is important to keep the questions flowing, to look interested and to be enthusiastic.

Remember, never be complacent as there is no guarantee you will get the job just because you get invited for a second or third interview with the same company:

- If your second or third interviews are with different people, treat each of the interviews as though you are visiting the company for the first time.
- Ask each person who interviews you plenty of questions, even if they are the same questions you have already asked a different interviewer. It is important to do this, or the second interviewer may say to the first that you were a quiet candidate who lacked interest in the role. This conclusion could be reached if you failed to ask enough questions, even ones you knew the answer to, during the second interview.
- You may have thought it unnecessary to ask questions the second time round because you knew the answers from the first interview with the first interviewer. But by not asking questions on each interview occasion, your interest levels may not be clear to both interviewers.
- The first interviewer will think you are outgoing and interested in the role because you did have questions to ask, but may then have fresh doubts about your application and suitability, and these will be based on the comments from the second interviewer.
- This could lead to the first and second interviewer disagreeing with each other about your application; as a result you may not get offered the job.

Companies like to feel that you will 'belong' to them. So, if you have dedicated interests outside work that have nothing to do with improving your skills in the workplace and a company deadline occurs that may mean you have to work an extra hour or so at the end of the day, you may need to give up those interests. Perhaps you are learning how to swim or play the guitar and the course is midweek? It might be an idea to move the course to a weekend. This is something you could possibly explain you would do if asked about your interests during an interview.

Avoid talking about any dangerous sports you may do in your spare time as this could go against your application, or any company insurances you may be eligible for. You will not come over as being macho or clever, just a potential liability. Give them up!

It is important to say only good things about your present and any previous employers. Company information is confidential, so remember this when you are giving your reasons for looking for new employment. If, for example, your present company is in financial difficulties, or your bosses don't get on and are always arguing, or your married boss is having an affair, or has a drink problem, keep this information or anything similar to yourself. Your reasons for looking for a new job should focus on just you.

During an interview, the interviewer will make a decision about you very quickly, so your application is less likely to be viewed favourably if you have said negative things about any of your present or previous employers, or colleagues for that matter. The interviewer will need to feel that you are trustworthy and loyal.

If, while being interviewed, you say that you are looking to leave your job because you have not been promoted, this could reflect badly on you. It could be that your attitude was wrong, and that you were therefore not suitable for promotion, or that your lack of experience meant you were not ready to be promoted.

Similarly, if a gripe with your salary is another reason for looking for a new job, a view may be taken that you were not worthy of the salary increase.

To talk about having a 'bad boss' or general disruption in the office is not a good thing to do either.

If you are leaving because you have a personality clash with your boss, don't mention this at an interview because it could come across that YOU are the one who might not be easy to get on with.

It is worth remembering that a lot of business owners know each other. Imagine you go for an interview with a company and the person conducting the interview knows people in your company, or indeed your boss. Aside from talking about the role in question, it might be that the interviewer is fishing for more information about the workings and client-base of your company, as well as general company information. The interviewer will not let on, and may be testing your level of loyalty; you will not necessarily be aware this is happening.

Stick to the golden rules, talk positively about the role you are doing in your present job, the vacancy, hobbies, interests, and relevant courses. When asked about your company, say it is a good place to work, but that you are ready to move on, or something similar.

A company may decide to offer you a video interview before taking steps to meet with you for a face-to-face interview. If this happens, follow the suggestions outlined throughout this book and make sure you are fully prepared in the same way you would be if you were having a face-to-face interview:

- It is important you check that all the equipment is working ahead of your interview, and that you log on a few minutes before it is due to start.
- Check your internet connection is stable, check the application you use for video conferencing is up to date, and check the microphone on your device works correctly so that the interviewer can hear you.
- Make sure the internet is free for your use during your video interview to ensure your connection on the video call remains consistent and is uninterrupted by bandwidth issues.
- Any technology that is not required for the interview should be turned off.
- Have a 'trial run' of yourself in the camera line to find your best angle.
- Avoid wearing heavy makeup, because a video interview can exaggerate the appearance of any makeup you have applied, especially to eyebrows, which if over-enhanced may come across as looking rather theatrical.
- Make sure your environment is tidy. The backdrop you decide to use may form part of the room you are sitting in for the interview, so make sure it is tidy and you can be clearly seen. Or, you may decide to use a virtual background; if so, keep it neutral.
- Dress smartly for your interview, in the same way you would for a face-to-face interview. Casual clothing, such as joggers or pyjama bottoms, will not be a good idea to wear, just in case you need to move away from the screen to fetch something, or even stand up!

- Dressing as though you are attending the interview face-to-face will make it easier for you to get into an interview mindset; this will help you deliver a better interview.
- Close the door so you have complete privacy and silence.
- Look directly into the camera as often as possible, to maintain eye contact.
- Avoid moving around too much.
- Have a notepad and pen/pencil with you.
- Have a copy of the job description near to your keyboard, as well as a copy of your CV. Video interviews can sometimes be more challenging than face-to-face interviews, which in turn can make it easy to forget dates, etc, on a CV. The interview circumstances will mean that it will be easy to discreetly have your CV near you.
- Have tissues handy, just in case.
- Have a glass of water available, but not too near to the keyboard, for obvious reasons!
- Well before your interview, ask a friend or family member to give you a video interview trial run so you know everything is working properly; they will also be able to check that you come across in the right sort of way too.

18   Marketing yourself

There could be some advantages if you choose to use a recruitment agency to help with your job search, but it is worth remembering that some organisations prefer not to use employment agencies when it comes to hiring new staff.

For this reason, you may decide to also apply directly to companies, so you do not miss out on job opportunities:

- By applying in response to an online advertisement.
- By targeting a select number of companies 'cold' that are growing and are of interest to you. Remember, not all organisations advertise their job opportunities.
- Or by using social media.

Remember to update your job history on LinkedIn so it mirrors your CV, and ensure any accolades, accomplishments or certifications are added to your LinkedIn Bio. You may also decide to add a video introducing yourself.

A hirer reviewing a candidate might look at social media platforms such as LinkedIn or even Facebook to marry up who they see at an interview and what is on their CV. They may use this alternative source of information about you for conversation during your interview!

Some companies may advertise their vacancies on job boards, or they may have job opportunities listed on their websites.

It is also possible to find out via comments posted on social media, who the best companies are to work for, so you could target them too.

Or they may invite people to submit CVs on a general basis by saying something like: *If you feel you have skills that could be of interest to our organisation, as well as an outgoing personality, then please email through your CV and a covering letter to hr@hr.com.*

Make sure you moderate any social media information you may have on yourself, because if you don't, too much of the wrong sort of information could work against you when it comes to job applications. There is always the possibility that a hirer may check you out before deciding whether to invite you in for an interview. If they see something about you that they do not like, or the information provided in your CV does not match what is on social media, you may miss out on an interview.

Always check your CV is up to date and that it includes a relevant profile for each role, as explained earlier. These days, there is no excuse for sending an out-of-date CV to a company. When it comes to targeting companies 'cold', try not to select too many companies at a time. Start with ten companies until you reach a satisfactory conclusion, then if necessary, target ten more. This will stop you from feeling disillusioned and may also prevent duplication and confusion.

- Keep a record of any comments, email responses or telephone conversations you may have with each company on file. This will give you a sense of progression.
- These days you may need to telephone a company to find out the correct email address for the person you will need to contact.
- When targeting a company 'cold', it is important to try and get the name of the person who might be responsible for receiving CVs.
- Some companies have quite detailed information on their websites with names, ranks and email addresses for key members of staff.
- Target an MD, CEO or Office Manager if an email address for HR is not available.

Your CV will need to have the desired effect, so the all-important covering letter will need to accompany it when it is sent out.

- As mentioned before, if you are sending your CV by email, make sure it goes off with a cover letter. The same should apply if it is being sent through via the company portal. It is good to get a delivery and read receipt too, if possible.

A cover letter is an important addition to have with your CV. It shows any company you are applying to how keen you are to secure a job. The cover letter will support your CV and give a strong indication of your interest in the opportunity. It will help highlight your relevant skills and give an idea of your levels of enthusiasm and capabilities. It will also emphasise your determination to get the role.

For example, you could start by saying how interested you are to apply for the position of Product Manager that you saw advertised on *The Guardian* online. It is important to adopt a direct approach as quickly as possible to show how serious and enthusiastic you are about the opportunity.

You can go on to talk about relevant experience you have gained in the workplace, and it would be good to emphasise the longevity you may have had in any of your roles. This will highlight that you are a stayer! Your positivity, how you can add value to the team, your transferable skills and willingness to learn will all be worth mentioning, and so will key achievements.

The content of the cover letter will vary according to your level and experience, but keep it to one page, whether you are at first job level, or senior management level. It should accompany your CV when you send it out.

Here is an example of a standard cover letter to accompany an emailed CV.

14 Sheep Way
Sotheby
SNR 1TR

mobile – 08777 555 000
email – hs@snailmail.com

Ms L Jones
Office Manager
Another Toy Company Ltd
Sotheby
SNX TLR

20 February 2020

Dear Ms Jones,

I am extremely keen to apply for the role of Marketing Account Manager that your company advertised in last Friday's edition of *The Daily News*.

The position you are advertising is of great interest to me because I have spent the last five years working as a Marketing Account Manager for Pre School Toys Limited and I have dealt with client budgets of more than £100k. Also, my greatest achievement was securing a TV marketing campaign which went on to generate an exclusive business deal with A&C Charter. Unfortunately, my company is relocating to Dubai so for this reason I am looking for a new position.

I am hardworking, resourceful and professional. I also enjoy dealing with clients and working to tight deadlines.

Please find attached a copy of my CV and I look forward to hearing from you at your earliest convenience.

Yours sincerely,

Harriet Smith

If you have applied 'cold' and you don't hear anything for a week or so, try telephoning the companies you have approached with your CV who have not responded to make sure your CV has been received, then wait.

Hopefully, you will eventually get positive replies. If you do not make progress where the companies you have targeted are concerned, then try approaching a fresh batch of companies.

If eventually a company you have approached yourself contacts you to invite you in for an informal interview, how do you handle the situation?

- Remember, any company that contacts you as a result of you contacting them, will have seen something on your CV that is of interest.
- The company may not have put together a job description; they may simply want to meet with you for an 'informal chat' to see whether your skills and personality are a good match for them. You may find that at such an early stage there is no indication of salary or duties.
- Try not to be put off. Be prepared to do a good pitch on yourself by treating the 'informal chat' as though it is an interview.
- Use the opportunity to really project yourself and your skills well. Do plenty of research and attend the 'informal chat' (interview) with *purpose.*

During the interview process, if you end up impressing the interviewers so much, it may be that the company will create a job description based on your skills and personality and present it to you.

The great thing is you will have got in before anyone else and, if you are suitable, the company may decide not to advertise the role and instead offer the position to you.

A salary might then be proposed; hopefully, if it is in line with your expectations, all should be concluded positively. Having said this, it is better to be flexible with your salary expectations and any overall duties that may be presented to you. That way you will stand a better chance of getting a firm job offer.

So, do not try and dictate salary terms, especially if you are currently unemployed, because this could potentially lose you the job offer. It is better to start working – after all, earning something of a salary is better than earning nothing. Forget the fact that the salary offer may be lower than what you were paid in your previous role. Take the job, prove yourself then get a salary increase. If you dither, someone else will snatch the opportunity from under your nose and you will be back to square one!

If you are out of work and you choose to hold out for the perfect salary in principle – say you were hoping for a salary of £35k and you have had a job offer at £30k to start immediately – it may be worth remembering that if you take the job at £30k, you might qualify for a salary increase after a few months which will take you closer to the salary you were hoping for in the first place. Please refer to the chapter on salary expectations.

If you decide against taking a job paying less than you were hoping for, you could spend another six months out of work. You would therefore have spent six months of your time earning nothing – you do the maths!

It is important to have a disciplined mind if you are out of work and looking for a job:

- You need to be mentally and physically prepared before starting the interview process.
- Cut back on eating comfort food, fry-ups, chips, chocolate, cakes, and the like. Eat healthy foods instead. It might be an idea to drink less alcohol too. If you do not belong to a gym because you cannot afford to pay the membership, then take up walking if you can. It is best to do some form of exercise, whatever you can manage.
- Aim to be fit and ready to Get That Job!
- Set aside an allocated number of hours each day for your job hunt.
- Try and be disciplined and get up early, at a fixed time.
- Maybe take a morning walk to get some air, then work on your applications and research for a couple of hours.
- Stop for lunch, then resume your search for a further couple of hours.
- Then switch off, and maybe take a further walk outdoors to clear your head, do something different for the rest of the late afternoon and evening so there is no danger you burn yourself out.

You may need to move away from home if you are having problems securing a job near to where you live. If this is the case, accommodation will be an important factor to consider:

- If you are going for interviews in a new area, for example you are thinking about relocating from Manchester to London, know where you will be living, because you will be asked this question at an interview.

- If possible, find a friend you can move in with who is within easy reach of where you will be attending your interviews. This will help a lot.
- Saying you will 'find somewhere to stay' if you get the job might not be enough to convince the interviewer that you will settle into the area and role.
- The interviewer will be more at ease with your application and relocation, knowing that you do have somewhere to stay.

Sometimes there can be the slimmest of differences between candidates. It may even be down to the location you live in that could be the deciding factor. It might be that the other candidate who can be specific about a relocation address will get offered the role if their skills and personality are similar.

If you have a quiet personality, it might be an idea to think about ways to try and boost your communication skills and confidence levels. For example:

- When you go shopping you could try talking to the cashier who may be serving you, even if you only mention the weather.
- If you find yourself in a crowded room and you do not know anybody, try initiating a conversation with the person next to you.
- So long as you are in a safe and secure environment, make the effort to create a conversation with someone whenever possible. This should help you feel more confident when speaking to people during an interview situation.
- If you have the funds, enrol on a weekend drama course.

It is important to do everything you can to project your personality during an interview, whatever the role.

As mentioned before, when doing research on companies, remember to gather as much information from company websites, the internet, company brochures and the press. A hirer can always tell if you have spent the right amount of time doing thorough research.

You may not necessarily get a job just because a friend or relative who works for the company you are applying to has put in a good word.

Always aim to get a job on your own merit.

19 Salary expectations

It is always best not to mention your salary expectations during an interview:

- Wait until the person who is interviewing you brings the subject up. If a salary is not mentioned, you should avoid saying anything.
- If you do get asked about your salary expectations, it is better not to say you need to earn a certain amount, then talk about your bills, rent, mortgage, etc.
- A salary is based on what the job is worth, and what you may be worth to any possible employer, not the cost of your monthly outgoings.
- You may be asked directly to give your salary requirements. If you are junior level, for instance, avoid saying you are looking for a fixed figure of £25k. Rather, say you are looking for a salary of 'around' £25k. Then if the role is paying £25k or £28k, you will not be too far off the mark. This will also apply if you are looking for a more senior role and your salary requirement is £60k, ask for 'around' £60k. Once again, if the role is paying £65k, you will not be too far off the mark.
- Try and show reasonable flexibility whether your salary expectations are at the higher level or more junior level.
- If the salary for the role is lower than you were hoping, avoid showing your disappointment; it is best not to say the salary is not enough.
- Do not be evasive or lie when you are asked about your earnings. You will get found out if you say your salary is more than it is.
- Do not dictate your salary requirements during an interview.
- The days of dictating salary requirements are over – this applies to most candidates who are looking for a job.

After interviews with other companies, the lower salaried role might be the very role you decide you like the most. So, if you dismiss the opportunity too quickly, it will be difficult to backtrack. You might not even be invited for a second interview because your attitude first time around regarding salary would have indicated disappointment. The company would presume you are no longer interested in the role:

- A good candidate will show interest in the role and avoid giving priority to the salary.
- Try to remain positive and focused because a lower salary can sometimes mean a better job.
- Try not to keep talking about how good you would be for the role and how much of an asset you would be to the company if you can't give solid examples of any relevant experience gained in previous roles. It is best not to blow your own trumpet just to try and prove you are worth a higher salary. In the end, if you are given the job, will you be able to do it effectively?
- If you start your new job on a slightly lower salary, you may be under less pressure to perform perfectly in your new role from day one. You may find you are able to settle into the role more easily and do the job better. Also, the right support is more likely to be at hand.
- You may also qualify for certain training courses, which could lead on to a more defined career opportunity.
- Sometimes the salary level does not always indicate greater job involvement.

A few years ago, there was little salary variation for similar roles. These days there can be a broad salary difference for similar roles. A lot will depend on the industry and success of the companies you may be applying to.

Tread with caution. People sometimes leave their jobs for the wrong reasons. For example, they may think they can get a better salary elsewhere, or they might simply feel they have been in a job for too long and resign from their position without having a job to go to.

With a false sense of security, they can hand in their notice expecting to walk into a new, better-paid job quickly and easily. Realising the toughness of the job market, they end up regretting their decision to leave their last job and have wanted it back. Only after going for job interviews elsewhere, then seeing their old job advertised, have they realised how good the opportunity they gave up really was.

20   References

Reference checks are a necessary part of the process.

You may get your job offer yourself without the help of a recruiter. Your prospective employer will then contact you directly to request references on you. Make sure anyone you choose to be your referee, whether they are giving a professional or personal reference, is credible and capable of providing the correct level of information about you.

It is important to remember to do the following:

- When you get a job offer, check the financial status of the company that is offering you the job before you accept it, especially if you are already in secure employment. You may be eager to move from your current company for career progression, but without realising, you could be joining a company that is financially unstable. Some hirers can be good at selling the dream during an interview, so if you don't thoroughly check the company you are thinking of joining, you may unexpectedly find yourself out of a job if the money isn't there to pay you.
- Make sure you receive your job offer/contract of employment, in writing before you give in your notice at work.

When seeking a new role, make sure that your referees are kept up-to-date with your job hunting situation and that they have given you permission to pass on their names and contact details to any company wishing to employ you. The following may apply:

- Once you have been offered a job, two references will be requested, or possibly three. This may depend on your level or the type of company that wishes to hire you.
- The prospective employer will contact your referees directly to request job/professional references from your line-manager, or HR

department. They may also request a personal reference from someone who knows you personally.

- You may be required to personally present proof of all your qualifications, formal or otherwise, as well as your ID (current passport/full driving licence).
- Make sure you have had recent dialogue with the people who will be giving you a reference, because you may need one quickly. This is important because your referees could quite easily be on holiday with no internet connection, have changed their mobile numbers, or be away from work and out of reach for some other reason.
- It is a must to have the current details of anyone who is providing a reference. Delayed access to professional and personal reference contacts can hold up the start date process.
- Keep checking to make sure any referee you give for a reference has not changed company.
- Make sure you have the right point of contact for reference requests, because sometimes they can only be generated by HR, especially where larger institutions such as banks are concerned.
- It is polite to keep your referees in the loop regarding any conclusive progress you make with your job hunting.

If you get a job via a recruiter and you provided the recruiter with referees for references that were carried out earlier in the recruitment process, before you secured your job, it is worth remembering that the reference checks on you might need to be repeated. Some companies like to do their own reference checking; the company you are joining may wish to contact you directly for names of referees so they can do their own reference checks on you.

Summary

Checklist for **How to Get That Job!**

Firstly, as you will have seen from Chapters 1 to 10 of this book, do everything necessary so you have the maximum chance of getting selected for an interview. To summarise, make sure you follow the key elements, which include:

CV profile	make sure it is targeted and relevant to the role in question
CV content	be truthful about your qualifications and experience
CV layout	keep it concise, well-organised and easy to read
Position	decide what role suits you and your circumstances best
Research	the companies that you are approaching
Practise	your interview techniques

Secondly, as covered more fully in Chapters 11 to 20 of this book, once selected for an interview, or interviews, make sure you are fully prepared, so you give yourself the best chance of success!

A checklist is useful to refer to before going for interviews, because when under pressure, it is easy to forget the most obvious things.

Please see some helpful reminders listed below:

- Make sure your suit or interview outfit is clean; if it is at the drycleaners, collect it well in advance
- Remember to check then polish your shoes (have a pair of spare laces if applicable just in case!)
- Make sure you have the company name, interview address, telephone number and directions
- Make sure you have the full name(s) of the interviewer(s)
- Have your CV in a folder in case you need to present it, as well as a copy of the job description because you may be asked to refer to it

- If applicable, have a portfolio containing some examples of your work
- It is always useful to take a pen or pencil and a small notepad
- Make sure your mobile phone is fully charged (and remember to switch it off before your interview)
- You may need to take your certificates
- Have your driving licence or passport with you, just in case
- Remember your train or bus pass
- Make sure you have sufficient fuel if you are using your vehicle
- It is always useful to have change, or other means to pay for parking
- Take some tissues or a handkerchief
- Take a small umbrella
- Remember to check your personal presentation
- Always allow plenty of time for travel so you arrive composed.

You will then be ready to get that job!

Once you get that job.

Remember, everyone has something to offer in the workplace. It doesn't matter if you are junior or senior level, or whether you have either a handful of GCSEs, or qualifications beyond a degree; seize whatever opportunity is presented to you at work and do everything you can to become a valued member of staff.

Make sure you:

- Work hard
- Avoid being the first to leave at the end of the day
- Avoid becoming complacent
- Keep up a smart dress code
- Are always on time
- Look interested
- Respect your boss
- Respect your colleagues

- Are a good team player
- Meet your deadlines
- Wait to be offered a salary increase

And hold on to that job!

Interview
Feedback

Notes